Animal Life

Funny & Weird

Land Mammals

Funny & Weird Animals Series

By

P. T. Hersom

This book is dedicated to my niece, Cecelia, and my nephew, Rylan, who live on a farm in Iowa. Animals are their game as they both help take care of chickens, cows and horses. Although mammals you will read about in my book may appear to be funnier and weirder than typical farm animals, they have experienced some of their own funny and weird mishaps such as being chased by the rooster all the way to the house, bucked off of their horse after a rabbit jumped out, and even thrown off of their calf (leave the bull riding to the cowboys kids). Not to mention, poop infested boots.

Love ya's, Cecelia & Rylan

Animal Life Funny & Weird Land Mammals

By P. T. Hersom

First Published, 2013

Printed in the United States of America

Hersom House Publishing

3365 NE 45th St, Suite 101, Ocala, Florida 34479 USA

Table of Contents

Mammal, what is a Mammal?

Mammals are animals, but not all animals are mammals. Clear as mud so far, right? Ok let's try again. Mammals have some things that make them special and different from other animals. Like three middle-ear bones, hair, and being warm-blooded. Reptiles like snakes and frogs on the other hand, are cold-blooded and birds of course have feathers instead of hair.

One other thing that female mammals have is mammary glands which are used to nourish their young with milk. In people, these are called breasts (such as, when a new born baby is being fed by its mother), with cows and goats they are called udders, and with other mammals such as cats and dogs, they're called teats or dugs.

And yes, you and I are mammals! The four characteristics that define mammals are that we have hair, we are warm-blooded, we have three middle-ear bones, and those of us who are female have breasts. Welcome to the mammal world. Being called a mammal seems kind of funny and weird doesn't it? However, it's the truth.

In this book we are going to be discovering funny and weird land mammals, but did you know there are also sea mammals, like the dolphin and whale? In addition, there are three types of mammals; the placentals, marsupials and monotremes.

Placental mammals are like us and have their young grow inside an embryonic organ called the placenta, which is attached to their mother's uterus, which is inside her tummy. Through this placenta, the unborn baby is fed nutrients and receives oxygen. Other examples of placental mammals are elephants, horses, dogs and cats.

Marsupial mammal babies are born very tiny and immature, and spend the first part of their lives growing inside their mother's pouch. Some popular marsupials are opossums, koalas and kangaroos.

Monotremes are the weirdest mammal, they lay eggs instead of giving birth to their young, just like a chicken! The duck-billed platypus and echidna are some monotreme mammals.

Mammals like to eat all kinds of different things. Like us, some eat both plants and meat, others eat meat only, and some only eat plants. While other mammals just eat insects. So let's go see!

Angora Rabbit

Where they live: Now a domestic breed found worldwide, originating from Angora, Turkey.

What they like to eat: Carrots of course and a high fiber diet with lots of water.

Tell Me More

Wouldn't you like to have one of these fluffy bunnies for your pet? Angoras are raised for their soft and silky wool which is even softer than cashmere. They get a haircut every 3 to 4 months, and their wool is sold and made into fine clothing. They came from Turkey along with the Angora goat and Angora cat, and became popular throughout Europe in the 18th century when the French royalty made them pets.

Even though, looking like a fur ball the cat coughed up with a face pasted on it, the Angoras are gentle and make wonderful indoor pets. Now that is one funny looking rabbit.

Aye-aye

Where they live: Madagascar, an island country off the coast of Southeastern Africa.

What they like to eat: Tree grubs, fruit, nectar, seeds and insects.

Tell Me More

This weird creature appears to be half cat and half vampire! However, it's actually part of the Lemur family of mammals. Besides having an unusual look, it also has a very unusual middle finger. This finger is extremely long and thinner than the others and has a ball and socket joint, much like our shoulder joint, which can rotate 360 degrees around.

Using its finger, the Aye-aye taps on wood searching for food like a woodpecker, up to eight taps per second. Once it discovers a hollow sound echoing back from the wood, they chew into the tree until a hole is opened, and then using its middle finger, poke into the hole stabbing grubs and insects. Humm... grub shish kabobs anyone?

Remember if a mammal gives you the middle finger, they may just be hungry.

Bearded Pig

Where they live: In the rainforest and mangroves of Borneo, Sumatra and the Malay Peninsula.

What they like to eat: Fruit, nuts, plants and roots.

Tell Me More

Step right up to see the "Bearded Pig Lady". Both the boys and the girls of this pig species have bushy hair along their nose and cheeks forming a wiry beard. Both sexes also possess long sharp tusks that can grow up to 10 in/25 cm in length and have powerful jaws that can crack open a coconut in one bite!

They are good swimmers and on many occasions spotted swimming between oceanic islands searching for new food sources. Like other pigs they spend the midday hanging out in the mud resting and sleeping, while looking for food in the morning and late afternoon when it's cooler.

Bongo

Where they live: Tropical jungles and forests of West, East and Central Africa.

What they like to eat: Leaves, shrubs, roots, fruits and grass.

Tell Me More

Bongos are part of the antelope family and have white stripes along their sides which help camouflage them in the jungle from predators. They are very shy, and when startled they run quickly into the dense jungle. While fleeing, they lay their horns on the back of their neck so they won't tangle in the surrounding jungle.

Both males and females have horns that are hollow inside and made of keratin on the outside. Keratin is the same material found in our hair, toenails and fingernails. I guess you could say, when you chew your fingernails, it's like a Bongo chewing its horns. Weird.

Brazilian Tapir

Where they live: Rainforest of South America.

What they like to eat: Leaves, plants, fruits and grass.

Tell Me More

Brazilian Tapirs can grow up to 8 ft/2.5 m in length and weigh up to 700 lb/317 kg, making them the second largest mammal in all of South America. They love to be around water and are good swimmers and divers! If a predator approaches, such as the jaguar, they will run into the water for safety and swim away. They have unique splayed toes, which help them navigate the muddy and soggy ground around rivers and waterways, three toes on both back feet and four toes on the front ones.

In Brazil they have been trained to pull plows and allow kids to ride them. Giddy up Tapir!

Emperor Tamarin

Where they live: In rain forest of the southwest Amazon Basin in Peru, Brazil and Bolivia.

What they like to eat: Flowers, insects, frogs, small birds, fruit, gum and snails.

Tell Me More

This little primate was named after the emperor of Germany, Wilhelm II. Who I guess also had distinctive mustache akin to the monkeys. They live in social groups of 8 to 20 monkeys, and are lead by a dominant female Tamarin, above the mature males.

Grooming each other for insects is an important bonding action done within the social group daily.

When a baby Tamarin is born it weighs a whopping 25% of its mother's weight! Wow. How would you like to have a baby that big Mom? They are carried around by their mother until they reach 70 days old, and then carried by others in the group until they reach 12 months old, at which point they can find insects and nourish themselves.

You can find Emperor Tamarins in the tree canopy of the tropical rainforest, generally located around the Amazon River Basin.

Gelada Baboon

Where they live: In the highlands of Ethiopia, in eastern Africa.

What they like to eat: Grass, flowers, bushes, thistles, fruits and roots.

Tell Me More

The Gelada Baboon lives in the highland areas of Ethiopia and is a grass grazing primate who mainly feeds on grass and plants. They are very social and live in communities made up of many bands. Not a rock band, but family bands, usually of one dominate male and multiple females and their young. While the bachelor males hang out in their own band.

During mating season the females have a bright red hairless patch of skin on their chest, which cues the males that love is in the air. Though very vocal, they communicate with facial gestures as well, such as sticking their tongue out, flipping their upper lip and making faces. Too funny!

Gerenuk

Where they live: In the desert and dry bush areas of East Africa.

What they like to eat: Leaves of trees and prickly bushes, flowers, fruit and plants.

Tell Me More

The name Gerenuk is from the Somali language and means "giraffe-necked", this why they are also called giraffe-necked antelope. Gerenuks are different from other antelope in the following ways; they seldom eat grass and generally do not drink water. It's not that they prefer drinking fruit punch over water; it's in what they like to eat.

Gerenuks feed on leaves of trees and bushes, by standing up on their hind legs and stretching their necks; they can reach higher into the vegetation than other animals and get the more tender shoots, flowers and fruit that are filled with moisture. This allows them to survive without water in the dry desert climate they live in.

Giant Panda

Where they live: In the mountain ranges of central China.

What they like to eat: Bamboo, grass, roots, rodents and birds.

Tell Me More

The Giant Panda is a bear and loves to eat bamboo. In fact, 99% of its diet is made of eating bamboo. They average in length up to 6 ft/1.8 m and may weigh up to 350 lb/ 160 kg, and have a very unique paw among bears. Their paw has 5 fingers and a thumb; this helps them hold on to the round bamboo as they eat it. Pandas on average eat 30 lb/14 kg of bamboo daily.

A mother may give birth to one or two cubs, and when born they are toothless, blind and pink. They are very tiny weighing around 4 oz/110 g and totally helpless, depending on their mother for food and protection until they reach six months old, when able to eat their own bamboo.

Hedgehog

Where they live: In New Zealand, Asia, Africa and Europe.

What they like to eat: Insects, snails, fruit, snakes, frogs, bird eggs and mushrooms.

Tell Me More

Similar in appearance to the porcupine, the Hedgehog may have up to 6500 spines covering its body and will roll into a ball when threatened. However, these spines do not easily come out and are actually hollow hair hardened with keratin. Remember keratin is the same material our hair, fingernails and toenails are made of.

Hedgehogs are fast runners, good swimmers and nocturnal, which means they like to play and look for food at night, covering up to 1.25 miles/2 km is common. Cute, cuddly and friendly these little ones make good pets too. Ouch! Watch out for the spines.

Koala

Where they live: Woodlands of Australia.

What they like to eat: Tree leaves, mainly of the Eucalyptus trees.

Tell Me More

Koalas, sometimes called Koala bears, not because they are bears, but because they look like the soft cuddly teddy bear from your bedroom, are leaf eating marsupials from Australia. A marsupial has babies born very tiny and immature, and spends the first part of their lives growing inside their mother's pouch.

A koala's baby is called a joey, born blind and furless, and only ¾ in/2 cm long, the joey will ride around with mom for the first year of its life, moving from her pouch, to ride on her belly and then her back.

During this time the joey gets nourishment from its mother's milk and "pap". Pap is a liquefied form of its mother's poop! Weird, huh. However this is good for the joeys' digestive system, by providing micro organisms that are necessary for digesting eucalyptus leaves.

Koalas spend most of their life in the canopy of the trees eating eucalyptus leaves which are very toxic and highly fibrous. They chew these leaves much like a cow chews its cud, by chewing and then swallowing the food, then regurgitates or burps it back up into their mouth to re-chew it.

This brings out additional energy from the leaves and assists in the digestive process. Koalas also are equipped with a longer intestine track than other mammals which helps break down the leaves, and their liver has the ability to detoxify the poisons.

The Koalas diet of leaves does not provide much energy so they spend much of their day sleeping, up to 20 hours a day. And since most of the leaves are high in water content the Koala doesn't need to drink water very often and may stay in the tree canopy for days before touching the ground.

Komondor

Where they live: Originally from Hungary, now found throughout the world.

What they like to eat: Dog food and Scooby snacks.

Tell Me More

The Komondor, also known as the "Mop Dog", for reasons that I think you can figure out, is a Hungarian breed of dog used for guarding livestock and property, and considered a Hungarian national treasure.

They are a large dog weighing up to 110 lb/50 kg and covered with a heavy, matted and corded coat. In the puppy stage their coat is fluffy and soft, and curls as the puppy grows up. As an adult their thick coat forms into cords, and protects them from predator bites, such as wolves. After a bath their coat takes over 2 days to dry! A good wet dog smell, nothing like it!

Long-necked Turtle

Where they live: Freshwater swamps and lakes of Australia.

What they like to eat: Fish, frogs, tadpoles, crayfish, clams, insects and worms.

Tell Me More

This funny looking turtle gets its name from its extremely long neck, which can even be longer than its shell. It's a kind of side-necked turtle, instead of pulling its neck directly backwards into its shell; it bends and folds it sideways into its shell.

It spends most of its day basking in the sun upon a rock or log, and when scared emits a foul smelling fluid from its musk glands. This stinky little habit has earned it another name, "Stinker" turtle. Have you ever had to "let out" a stinker?

Mandrill

Where they live: In tropical rainforest of equatorial Africa: the Congo, Gabon and Cameroon.

What they like to eat: Fruit, reptiles, roots and insects.

Tell Me More

These guys look like they fell asleep at the wrong party and woke up with their butt and face painted. However, these extraordinary colored Mandrills are the real thing, with red and blue skin on their faces and backside. They're equipped with scary large canine teeth that may be displayed for self-defense, but are more commonly bared for friendly social communication.

Mandrills are the largest monkey in the world and may weigh up to 100 lb/46 kg and live in social groups called "hordes". These hordes may be made up of hundreds of individuals; the largest recorded horde had over 1300 Mandrills.

They spend most of their day on the ground looking for food, but will search to the top of the tree canopy for food too. Built into the cheeks of their mouth are little pouches, snack holders, which they store food in to snack on later. At night Mandrills sleep in the trees and each night they will sleep in a different tree.

Okapi

Where they live: In the Ituri Rainforest of the Democratic Republic of the Congo, in Africa.

What they like to eat: Tree leaves and buds, fruits, ferns, grass and mushrooms.

Tell Me More

Even though the Okapi appears to be related to the zebra because of its black and white strips, it's actually closer to the giraffe. Their body shapes are very similar to the giraffe's except their neck is much shorter and both have long tongues growing up to 14 in/35 cm long, which they use to strip leaves from tree branches. The Okapi's tongue is so long they can even touch their own forehead and clean out their ears with it!

They stand about 6 ½ ft/2 m tall at their shoulders and weigh around 750 lb/340 kg. Images of the animal have been discovered on ancient Egyptian carvings and on the front of a great Persian hall from the fifth century BC. However, this mysterious creature only became known to modern science in 1901, when discovered by British explorer, Sir Harry Johnston with the help of African pygmies.

Platypus

Where they live: Australia.

What they like to eat: Insect larvae, clams, crayfish, freshwater shrimp and worms.

Tell Me More

The Platypus is so unusual and funny looking, that English scientists in the 18th century upon seeing a specimen of the animal thought it was a joke or prank, and done by a skilled taxidermist (a taxidermist is a person who stuffs dead animals for display). For it had the bill of a duck for a nose, the body and tail like a beaver and webbed feet like that of an otter. It was the weirdest animal they had ever seen!

The Platypus' weirdness did not stop with its funny looks; they soon discovered the Platypus is one of only five mammals in the world that lay eggs instead of giving birth to their young. And that they are part of few mammals worldwide that are venomous!

The male Platypus has a spur on its hind foot, as shown in the picture above, which can deliver a venomous strike against a threatening predator. This venom is not deadly to people, but can cause terrible pain.

The Platypus is a good swimmer and spends most of the day sleeping in a burrow usually dug into the side of a river bank. Then in the evening it will hunt for food in the water. It loves to find things to eat in the muddy bottom, such as greyfish, shrimp or worms. Without using its eyes or feet, the Platypus instead uses its highly sensitive duck-billed snout, which is capable of detecting tiny muscle movement of its prey through electro-receptors.

If you had a chance to touch its snout you would find out that it's not hard, but soft and pliable, and rubbery. Oh and did I mention they have no teeth? Why do you think "Perry the Platypus", the cartoon character on the show "Phineas and Ferb" never smiles?

Proboscis Monkey

Where they live: Mangrove and rainforest near rivers in Borneo, an island in Southeast Asia.

What they like to eat: Fruit, leaves, seeds, flowers and insects.

Tell Me More

Who said size doesn't matter? With the Proboscis Monkey, also called the Long-nosed Monkey, the bigger the nose the male has, the more females are attracted to him. Scientists think the larger nose causes enhanced monkey calls to the females.

As an infant the nose is much smaller but continues to grow as the young monkey matures into an adult until the nose completely covers the chin. Now that's a big nose!

These monkeys spend a lot of their time around rivers and are very good swimmers, with webbed feet and the ability to swim up to 65 ft/20 m underwater! During the middle of the day they will look for food more inland and then towards evening return to the river area and sleep in the trees near the river at night.

Ring-tailed Lemur

Where they live: Madagascar, an island country off the coast of Southeastern Africa.

What they like to eat: Leaves, fruit, flowers, herbs, insects, sap and tree bark.

Tell Me More

You may recognize these little guys from the movie "Madagascar", where King Julien XIII is a Ring-tailed Lemur. Not only popular in movies but very social too, Ring-tails live in groups called troops of up to 25 individuals, and have a dominant female leader. I guess you could call her the "Queen" of the troop. The troop spends most of its day on the ground hunting for food; however, they are also very good tree climbers.

A weird thing the males do during mating season is to have a "Stink Fight", to chase off the other boys from the girls. The stink fight begins by rubbing their wrist glands against their tails which creates a smelly, stinky odor bad enough to knock your socks off. Then they swing their tails at one another, and the male with the stinkiest tail wins the stink fight.

In the cool early part of the day the Ring-tailed Lemur may be found sun worshipping. They like to warm themselves up by sunbathing in the sun. The usual sunning position is taken by sitting on its butt, with legs stretched outward facing the sun. This warms up their tummy area where the fur is not as thick.

At night the troop will break up into sleeping parties, huddling close up for warmth.

Saiga Antelope

Where they live: In grasslands of Russia, Kazakhstan and Western Mongolia.

What they like to eat: Shrubs, herbs and grasses.

Tell Me More

No these photos have not been altered, even though it looks like someone pasted a partial elephant's trunk on their face! The Saiga Antelope is a critically endangered species, and may be why you have never seen one before; at least I hadn't until researching for this book.

The Saiga is a smaller, stocky antelope that moves from place to place in search of food and migrates in the summer from grassy pastures to winter grasslands in desert regions. During the mating season called the "rut", the males fight over the females by head butting each other. These fights can be very tiring on the animals and can even cause death. In fact, 90% of the males during this rut period will die from exhaustion from all the fighting. Weird, but not funny.

Scimitar-horned Oryx

Where they live: Formerly North Africa, now extinct in the wild.

What they like to eat: Grass, plants, roots, buds, shrubs and fruit.

Tell Me More

Now only found in managed reserves the Scimitar-horned Oryx was over hunted for their horns, meat and robust hide. Once roaming in large herds throughout the North African desert regions, their bodies are well equipped to handle the hot desert temperatures that would kill most mammals. Having the ability to reach a body temperature of 115 F/46.5 C before sweating and special kidneys that minimize the need to go potty, they can go without water for up to 10 months!

In ancient Egypt the Oryx were tamed like cows and used for religious ceremonies and food. In addition, a Scimitar-horned Oryx may have been the mythical one-horned unicorn! From side angles they appear to only have one horn, plus their horns are hollow and do not grow back if broken off. So if one was lost, it would only have one horn the rest of its life.

Sloth

Where they live: In trees in the jungles of South and Central America.

What they like to eat: Leaves, buds, insects and reptiles.

Tell Me More

The Sloth is a tree dwelling animal that moves very slowly due to its diet of low nutrition tree leaves. This food source provides little energy and takes days for the Sloth's digestive system to process completely, which may take up to a month. Therefore, they only poop about once a week!

Sloths have long curved claws on their hands and feet which help them hang upside down from branches, which they love to do. Usually eating, sleeping and even giving birth to their babies while hanging from tree limbs. Sloths while on the ground move at the lightning fast speed of 6.5 ft/2 m a minute. So they only hit the ground to look for a mate, go to the potty, or to move to another tree for food.

Since they hang upside down so much of the time, their hair grows in the opposite direction of most mammals, and provides a home for many strange things like beetles, moths, fungi, algae and even cockroaches! Now that's weird!

Star-nosed Mole

Where they live: Wetlands of Eastern Canada and Northeastern United States.

What they like to eat: Worms, insects, small fish, slugs and snails.

Tell Me More

Easily identified by the 22 pink fleshly feeler things around its snout, called Eimer's organs, it has more than 25,000 tiny sensory receptors, which the Star-nosed Mole uses to feel its way around. Since they're functionally blind (meaning they couldn't pass an eye examine even if their life depended on it), they use their star nose to find food and have been labeled the fastest eating mammal on earth, by identifying and eating prey within 120 milliseconds!

These hamster sized moles are good swimmers and can smell underwater by exhaling air bubbles onto objects, and then breathe the air bubbles back in through their nose. Like other moles they dig tunnels in the ground hunting for food, but different from other moles, often under a stream or pond with the tunnel exiting into the water.

Sun Bear

Where they live: In the tropical forest of Southeast Asia.

What they like to eat: Honey, honeycombs, insects and fruit.

Tell Me More

If you think this bear has a funny long tongue, you're right! The Sun Bear's tongue can extend up to 10 in/25 cm beyond its mouth, which it uses to extract insects from trees and honey from beehives. Known by its crescent shaped colored patch on its chest which ranges in color from golden to a pale white, the Sun Bear is the smallest of all the bears on earth.

Having slightly turned in large paws, with long curved claws make the Sun Bear a very good tree climber, and these natural tools are used to tear open fallen logs to find insects to eat. Sun Bears live in a warm tropical climate year around, so they do not hibernate like other bears do.

Vampire Deer

Where they live: Native to Korea and China.

What they like to eat: Wetland plants and grasses.

Tell Me More

The Vampire Deer has no antlers, but instead as been equipped with two large canine teeth forming curved tusks, that protrude out of their mouth like vampire fangs! These tusks grow up to 3 in/ 8 cm long and can be pulled back with the face muscles when eating or thrust outward when challenged by another male deer making the tusks appear longer and scary. Arrrr...!

This deer is also known by the name "Water Deer" because it lives around wetland marshes alongside rivers hiding in the tall rushes and reeds. They are good swimmers and often swim to river islands that may be several miles from the river's edge.

Wallaby

Where they live: Australia and New Guinea.

What they like to eat: Leaves, vegetables and grasses.

Tell Me More

Wallabies look like their larger cousin the Kangaroo and too, are marsupial mammals, raising their babies called "joeys" within their mothers pouch. The male Wallaby is called a"jack" and the female a "jill", so with jack and jill and joey we have a Wallaby family group called a troupe!

They can jump fast and high because of their powerful hind legs, and can give predators good swift kicks too. With their long, strong tail, they support and balance themselves, and with one quick whip of their tail can hurt an attacking enemy. Fighting or "boxing" happens among jacks in pursuit for the jills, during the mating season. Funny!

What Did You Learn Today? Questions

1. The Angora rabbit can look like a giant fur ball, true or false?

2. I have an extremely long middle finger I use for getting food. What is my name?

3. The Bearded Pig must shave once a week, true or false?

4. Does the Bongo antelope have spots on its back?

5. Is the Brazilian Tapir found in North America or South America?

6. The Emperor Tamarin monkey has a long curly mustache, true or false?

7. I communicate by sticking out my tongue and making faces. What is my name?

8. True or false, the Gerenuk antelope likes to eat standing up on its hind legs?

9. Does the Giant Panda love to eat peanut butter?

10. Can the Hedgehog make a cute, cuddly pet?

11. Koalas are part of the teddy bear family of mammals, true or false?

12. My name is Komondor and I'm a Hungarian national treasure. Am I a cat or dog?

13. I'm a Long-necked Turtle with something so long it won't fit into my shell. What is it?

14. My butt and face look like they were painted with bright colors. What is my name?

15. The Okapi's tongue is so long they can clean their own ears with it, true or false?

16. The Platypus has a bill like a duck, does it quack too?

17. The Proboscis Monkey has a "crazy big" nose, true or false?

18. I'm from Madagascar and I like to sunbathe and get my tummy tan. What is my name?

19. The Saiga Antelope is half elephant and half antelope, true or false?

20. Can the Scimitar-horned Oryx go without water for 10 months?

21. What animal spends most of its time hanging upside down and only poops once a week?

22. This little animal was born a "star" and likes to dig tunnels. What is it?

23. Do Sun Bears hibernate like other bears?

24. Does the Vampire Deer like to suck blood?

25. Wallabies live around the Great Wall in China, true or false?

What Did You Learn Today? Answers

1) True.

2) Aye-aye.

3) False, they do not shave at all, but they do have a beard.

4) No, they have stripes on their back.

5) In South America where the country of Brazil is located.

6) True.

7) The Gelada Baboon.

8) True.

9) No, it loves to eat bamboo!

10) Yes.

11) False, Koalas are not bears at all, not even a teddy.

12) The Komondor is a dog, also called the Mop Dog.

13) My neck, it is so long that I bend it and fold it sideways underneath my shell.

14) Mandrill.

15) True.

16) No.

17) True, its nose gets so big it covers its chin!

18) The Ring-tailed Lemur.

19) False, even though its nose looks part elephant.

20) Yes.

21) The Sloth.

22) The Star-nosed Mole.

23) No.

24) No, but it does have large fangs!

25) False, they live in Australia and New Guinea.

Other Books to Enjoy by P. T. Hersom

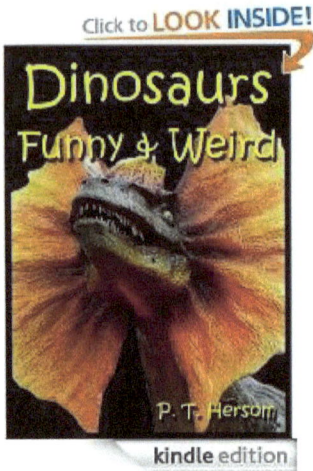

Dinosaurs Funny & Weird Extinct Animals

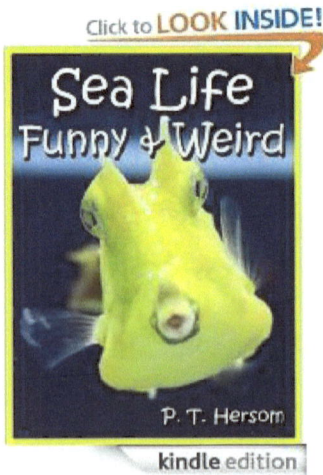

Sea Life Funny & Weird Marine Animals

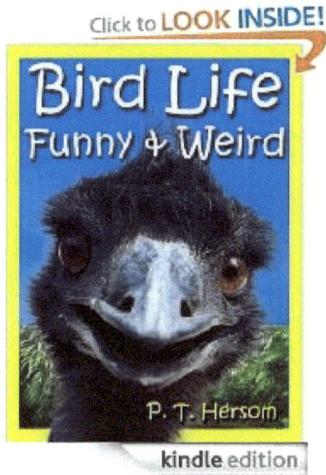

Bird Life Funny & Weird Feathered Animals

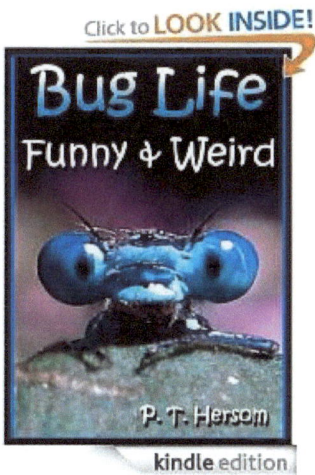

Bug Life Funny & Weird Insect Animals

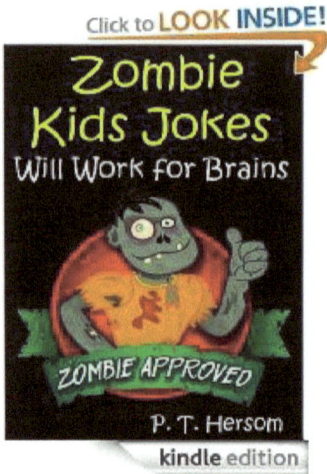

Zombie Jokes: Will Work for Brains

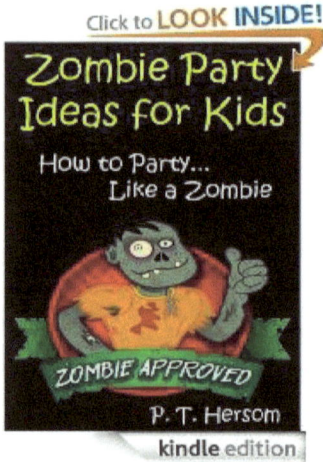

Zombie Party Ideas for Kids: How to Party Like a Zombie

Enjoyed the Book?

Thank you for buying this book. I hope that you and your children enjoy reading the book and learning about the animals in the book as much as I did writing it. If you found the book enjoyable, please help me out by posting a review on the Amazon page. Thank you for taking the time to do so. It is very much appreciated.

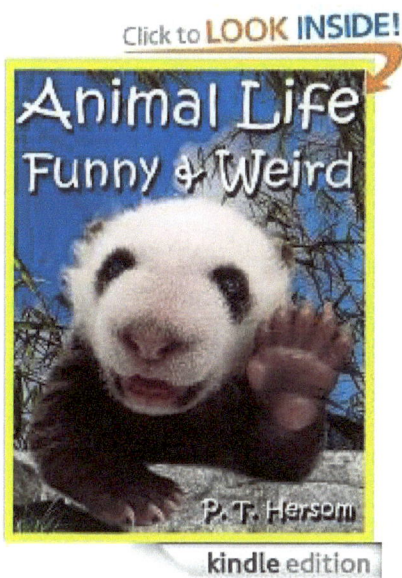

www.ingramcontent.com/pod-product-compliance
Lightning Source LLC
Chambersburg PA
CBHW041358090426
42741CB00001B/15